Write the missing capital and lowercase letters.

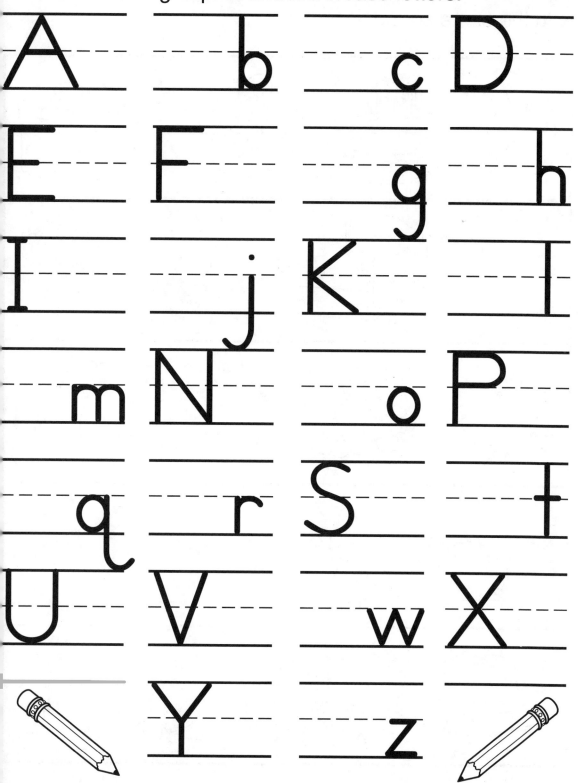

A   b   c   D

E   F   g   h

I   j   K   I

m   N   o   P

q   r   S   t

U   V   w   X

Y   z

1

Circle the two pictures in each row whose names **begin** with the same sound.

Look at the pictures. Write the letter you hear at the **beginning** of each word.

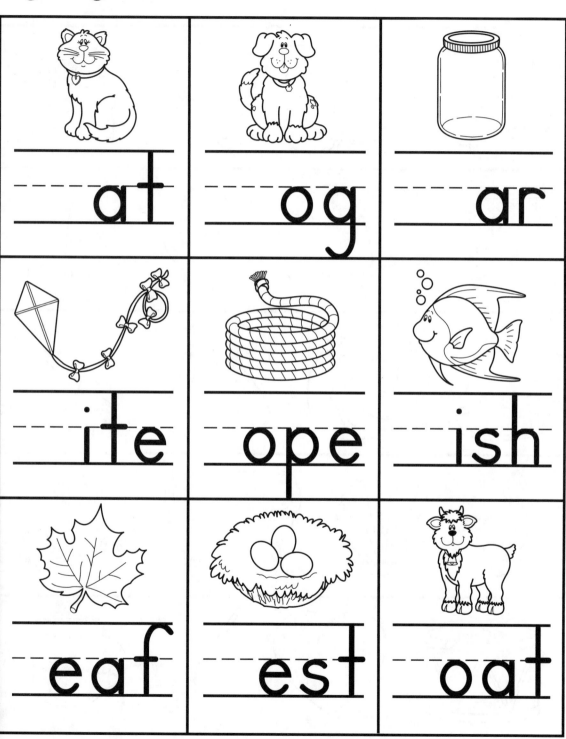

at   og   ar

ite   ope   ish

eaf   est   oat

Circle the two pictures in each row whose names **end** with the same sound.

Look at the pictures. Write the letter you hear at the **end** of each word.

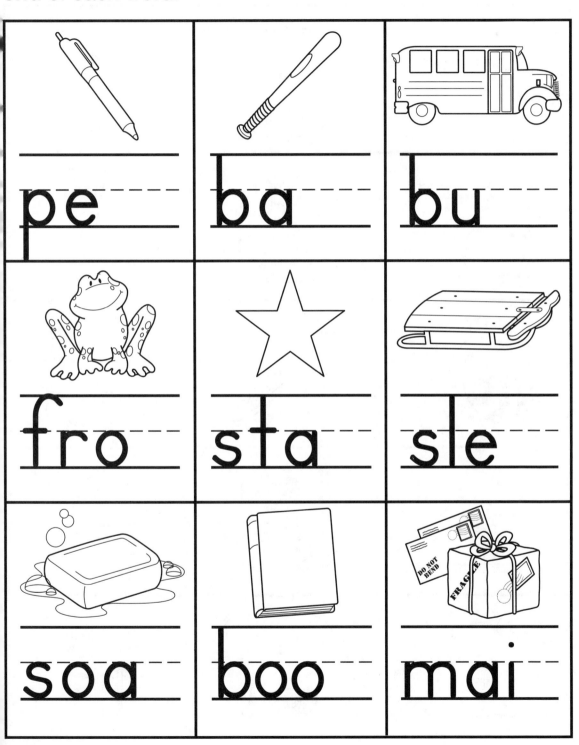

pe   ba   bu

fro   sta   sle

soa   boo   mai

Circle the two pictures in each row whose names **rhyme**.

Look at the pictures in each box. Write the beginning letter of each word to complete the word family.

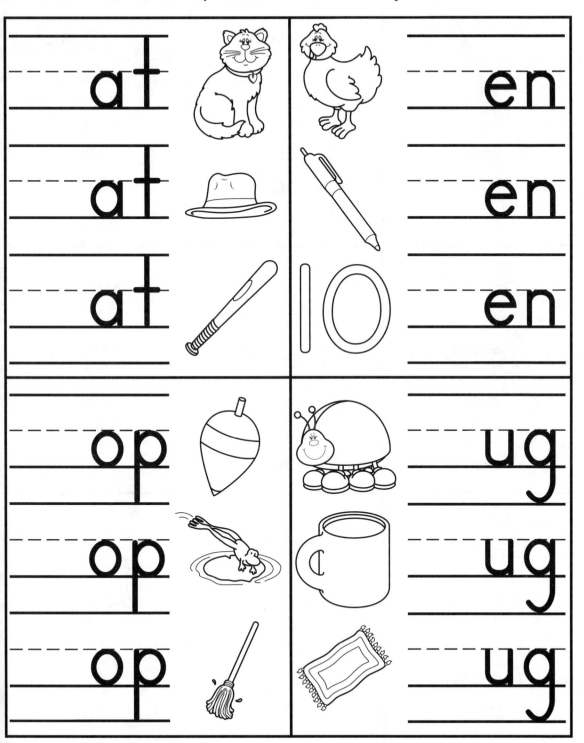

Fill in the circle next to the word that matches each picture.

○ map	○ bun	○ car
○ mop	○ sand	○ cow
○ man	○ sun	○ can
○ bell	○ book	○ rake
○ wall	○ hook	○ cake
○ ball	○ back	○ cape
○ clock	○ sat	○ horse
○ clown	○ stop	○ horn
○ coat	○ star	○ house

Circle the word that matches each picture.

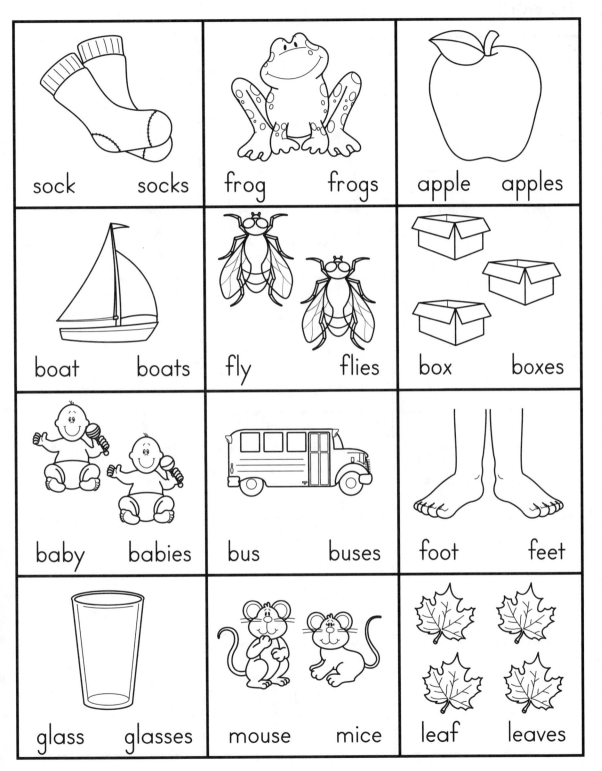

sock socks	frog frogs	apple apples
boat boats	fly flies	box boxes
baby babies	bus buses	foot feet
glass glasses	mouse mice	leaf leaves

Look at each picture. Write the missing vowel to complete the word.

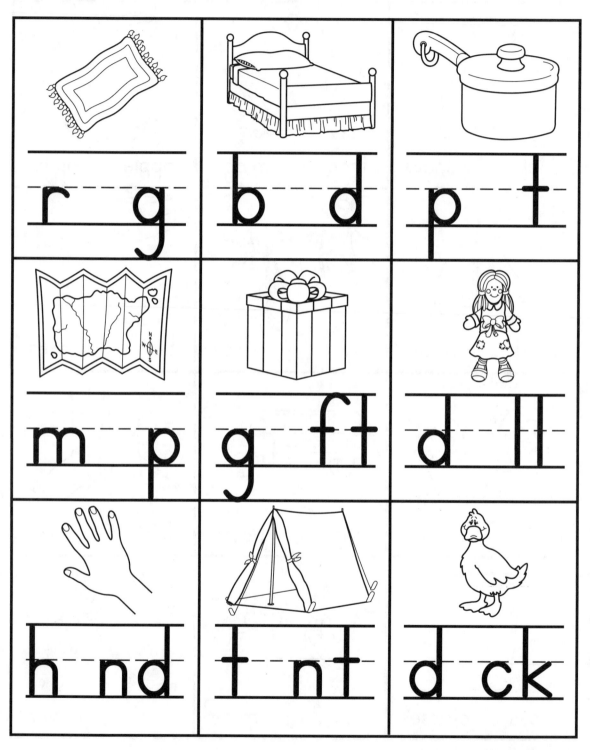

r __ g   b __ d   p __ t

m __ p   g __ ft   d __ ll

h __ nd   t __ nt   d __ ck

Circle the words in each row that have the long vowel sound shown.

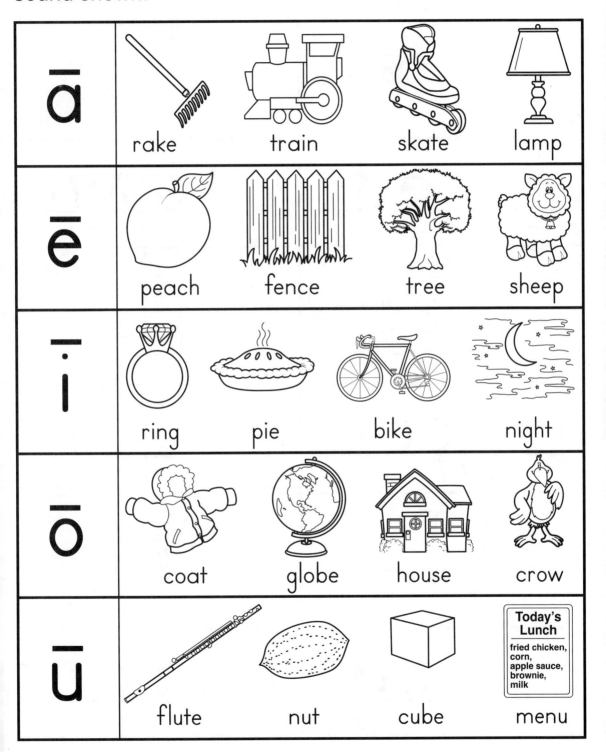

ā	rake	train	skate	lamp
ē	peach	fence	tree	sheep
ī	ring	pie	bike	night
ō	coat	globe	house	crow
ū	flute	nut	cube	menu

Today's Lunch

fried chicken, corn, apple sauce, brownie, milk

Write the missing blend: **pl**, **cl**, **fl**, **gl**, **bl**, or **sl**.

 ed

own

ock

ue

ag

ant

Write the missing blend: **br**, **cr**, **dr**, **fr**, **gr**, or **tr**.

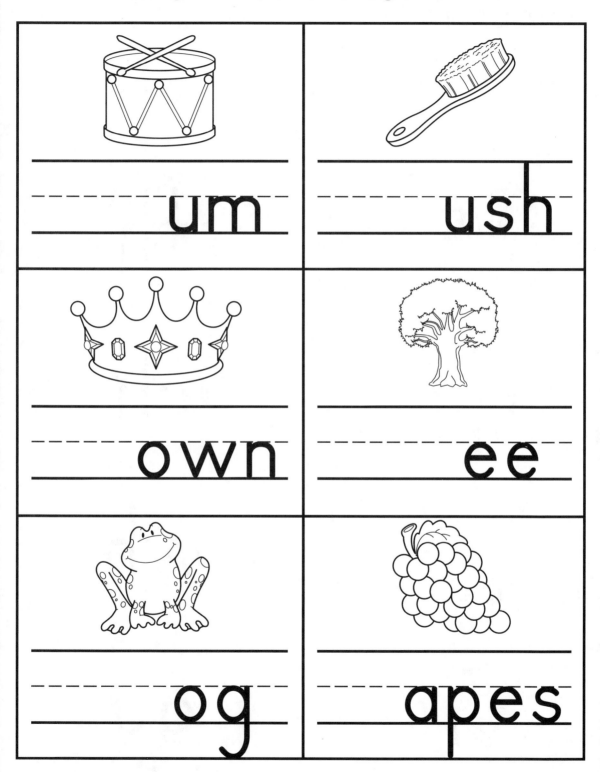

_____ um

_____ ush

_____ own

_____ ee

_____ og

_____ apes

Draw a line from each picture to the letters that make its beginning sound.

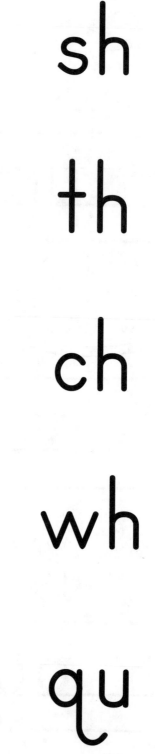

sh

th

ch

wh

qu

Circle the correct word to complete each sentence.

1. She is _____ a book. (read, reading)

2. I like to _____ games. (play, playing)

3. We _____ to school today. (walked, walking)

4. The rain is _____ down hard. (coming, come)

5. I need to _____ my room. (clean, cleaned)

6. I _____ the ball at practice last night. (kick, kicked)

7. He _____ me wash the dishes. (helping, helped)

8. The cat is _____ in the sun. (sleep, sleeping)

Write the correct contraction from the word list for each pair of words.

1. I   am

_____

- - - - - - - - - - - - - - - -

_____

Word List
it's
won't
I'm
can't
they're

2. can   not

_____

- - - - - - - - - - - - - - - -

_____

3. it   is

_____

- - - - - - - - - - - - - - - -

_____

4. they   are

_____

- - - - - - - - - - - - - - - -

_____

5. will   not

_____

- - - - - - - - - - - - - - - -

_____

Circle the correct pronoun to complete each sentence.

1. Deshana likes sports.

   _____ is good at soccer.   (It, She)

2. Jim and Rico play basketball.

   _____ are on the same team.   (They, We)

3. My sister and I are learning tennis.

   _____ are beginners.   (He, We)

4. Hayley got a new baseball bat.

   _____ is made of wood.   (She, It)

5. Karl joined the football team.

   _____ is a kicker.   (He, They)

Draw a line from a word on the left to a word on the right to make a compound word for each picture.

air   flake

base   paper

chalk   fish

mail   board

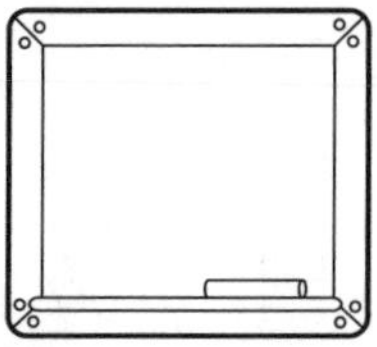

news   ground

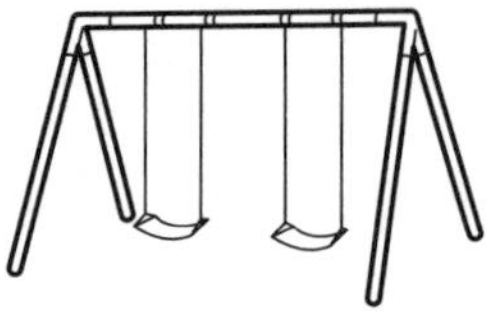

play   ball

snow   box

star   plane

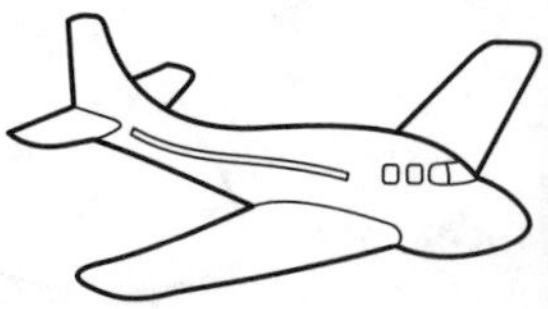

Draw a line from each word to its opposite.

happy	little
big	right
up	slow
left	off
fast	under
hot	sad
on	cold
over	down

Draw a line from each word to a word that means about the same thing.

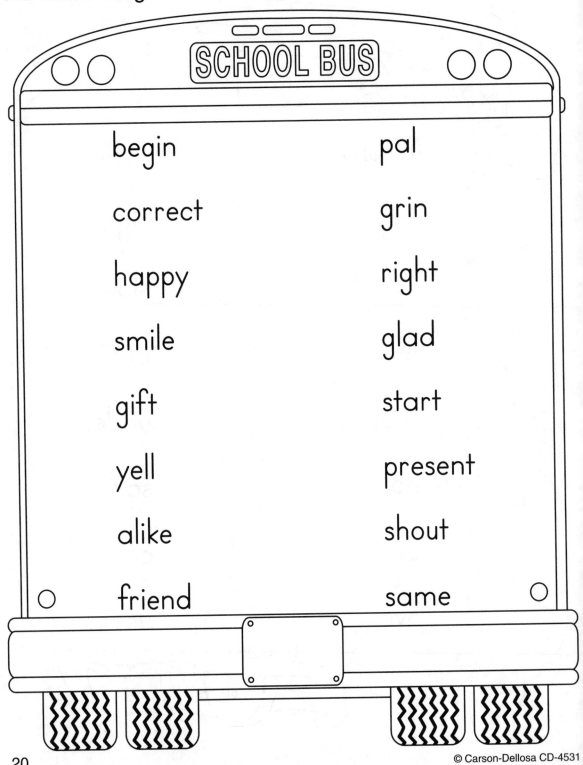

SCHOOL BUS

begin	pal
correct	grin
happy	right
smile	glad
gift	start
yell	present
alike	shout
friend	same

Write the words from the list in alphabetical order.

frog

up

man

jump

apple

sun

door

Circle the picture in each box that goes with the sentence.

The frog likes to jump.

The snowman has a sled.

The girl has a lunch box.

The penguin is skating.

22

Unscramble each group of words to make a sentence.

1. The   sleeping.   is   cat

_____

- - - - - - - - - - - - - - - - - - - -

_____

_____

2. the   is   He   rug.   on

_____

- - - - - - - - - - - - - - - - - - - -

_____

_____

3. is   name   Cookie.   His

_____

- - - - - - - - - - - - - - - - - - - -

_____

_____

4. wake   Don't   up.   him

_____

- - - - - - - - - - - - - - - - - - - -

_____

_____

Circle the correct punctuation mark for each sentence.

1. We went sailing   .   ?

2. The wind was strong   .   ?

3. Have you ever been sailing   .   ?

4. Our boat had two sails   .   ?

5. Do you like boats   .   ?

6. We saw many other boats   .   ?

7. I had a good time   .   ?

8. When will we go again   .   ?

Number each sentence to show the correct order.

Finally, I rake the leaves into a pile again!

First, I rake all of the leaves into a pile.

Next, my friend jumps into the leaf pile.

Look at the picture of the book, then answer the questions.

The Busy Bee
by Jane Honey

Illustrated by
Doug Buzz

1. What is the title of this book?

_____

_____

_____

2. Who is the author of this book?

_____

_____

_____

3. Who drew the pictures in this book?

_____

_____

_____

If a sentence tells about something that could really happen, color the picture. If it could not happen, draw an X on the picture.

1. We played a game.

2. The girl rakes leaves.

3. A bird can fly.

4. A boy can fly.

5. Penguins play hockey.

6. The boy won the race.

7. The class took a test.

8. Beavers brush their teeth.

Read the story and answer the questions.

Kim went for a walk. She saw a lot of birds. She jumped over a rock. Then, she picked up two orange leaves. Kim had fun, but now it was time to go home.

1. Where did Kim go?

_____

- -

_____

2. What did Kim see?

_____

- -

_____

3. What did Kim pick up?

_____

- -

_____

Draw a line to match each cause with an effect.

James found the cereal.

He read a story.

James studied for a test.

He went to bed.

James picked out a book.

He ate breakfast.

James was tired.

He got a good grade.

Read each story and fill in the circle beside the main idea.

1. José and Derrick went to the mall. They bought new shoes. They ate pizza for lunch before going home.

   ○ José and Derrick went to the mall.
   ○ José and Derrick ate pizza for lunch.
   ○ José and Derrick bought new shoes.

2. Leah and Amy played on the swings and in the sand. They fed the ducks. Leah and Amy had fun at the park.

   ○ Leah and Amy played on the swings.
   ○ Leah and Amy had fun at the park.
   ○ Leah and Amy fed the ducks.

3. Tara and Tim went to the beach. They found shells and played in the sand. They also went swimming.

   ○ Tara and Tim went swimming.
   ○ Tara and Tim played in the sand.
   ○ Tara and Tim went to the beach.

30

First Grade Activities Answer Key

Page 1
A capital or lowercase letter should be printed for each letter of the alphabet.

Page 2
The following pictures should be circled:
- First row: moon and mouse
- Second row: bed and bee
- Third row: sun and sock
- Fourth row: turtle and top
- Fifth row: hat and house

Page 3
Beginning letters should be written to make the following words:

cat	dog	jar
kite	rope	fish
leaf	nest	goat

Page 4
The following pictures should be circled:
- First row: train and spoon
- Second row: net and boat
- Third row: bell and snail
- Fourth row: tub and crab
- Fifth row: drum and broom

Page 5
Ending letters should be written to make the following words:

pen	bat	bus
frog	star	sled
soap	book	mail

Page 6
The following pictures should be circled:
- First row: tag and flag
- Second row: cake and rake
- Third row: bee and key
- Fourth row: lamp and stamp
- Fifth row: bear and chair

Page 7
Beginning letters should be written to make the following words:

cat	hen	top	bug
hat	pen	hop	mug
bat	ten	mop	rug

Pages 8
The following words should be selected: mop, sun, car, ball, book, cake, clown, star, and horse.

Page 9
The following words should be circled: socks, frog, apple, boat, flies, boxes, babies, bus, feet, glass, mice, and leaves.

Page 10
Vowels should be written to make the following words:

rug	bed	pot
map	gift	doll
hand	tent	duck

Page 11
The following words should be circled: rake, train, skate; peach, tree, sheep; pie, bike, night; coat, globe, crow; flute, cube, menu.

Pages 12-13
Beginning blends should be written to make the following words:

sled	clown
block	glue
flag	plant
drum	brush
crown	tree
frog	grapes

© Carson-Dellosa CD-4531

A

Page 14

sh

th

ch

wh

qu

Page 15

1. reading   2. play
3. walked   4. coming
5. clean   6. kicked
7. helped   8. sleeping

Page 16

1. I'm   2. can't   3. it's
4. they're   5. won't

Page 17

1. She   2. They   3. We
4. It   5. He

Page 18

Lines should be drawn to make the following words: airplane, baseball, chalkboard, mailbox, newspaper, playground, snowflake, and starfish.

Page 19

Lines should be drawn between the following words: happy/sad, big/little, up/down, left/right, fast/slow, hot/cold, on/off, and over/under.

Page 20

Lines should be drawn between the following words: begin/start, correct/right, happy/glad, smile/grin, gift/present, yell/shout, alike/same, and friend/pal.

Page 21

Words should be in order as follows: apple, door, frog, jump, man, sun, up.

Page 22

The frog likes to jump.

The snowman has a sled.

The girl has a lunch box.

The penguin is skating.

Page 23

1. The cat is sleeping.
2. He is on the rug.
3. His name is Cookie.
4. Don't wake him up.

Page 24

Sentences 1, 2, 4, 6, and 7 need a period (.); sentences 3, 5, and 8 need a question mark (?).

Page 25

1. First, I rake all of the leaves into a pile.
2. Next, my friend jumps into the leaf pile.
3. Finally, I rake the leaves into a pile again!

B

Page 26
1. The Busy Bee
2. Jane Honey
3. Doug Buzz

Page 27
Pictures 1, 2, 3, 6, and 7 should be colored; pictures 4, 5, and 8 should have an X drawn on them.

Page 28
1. Kim went for a walk.
2. Kim saw birds, a rock, and leaves.
3. Kim picked up two orange leaves.

Page 29

Page 30
1. José and Derrick went to the mall.
2. Leah and Amy had fun at the park.
3. Tara and Tim went to the beach.

Pages 31-32
Shapes should be colored or written on according to the directions. The total number of triangles is 3 (page 32).

Page 33

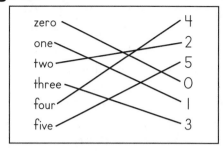

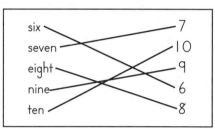

Page 34
Dots should be connected in order from 0 to 50 to form a kangaroo.

Pages 35-37
Missing numbers should be filled in.

Page 38
1. circle   2. flower   3. pumpkin
4. bunny   5. pizza

Page 39
Lines should be drawn from each fish to the appropriate word. Fish should be colored according to the directions.

Page 40
A. 34   B. 51   C. 77
D. 13   E. 68   F. 80

Page 41
B, E, F, H, I, J, L, M, and P should be >;
A, C, D, G, K, N, and O should be <.

Page 42
A. 6   B. 9   C. 10
D. 7   E. 10

C

Page 43

A. 9   B. 6   C. 9
D. 9   E. 4   F. 9
G. 9   H. 9   I. 6
Six suns should be colored.

Page 44

A. 7   B. 8   C. 4   D. 6
E. 9   F. 6   G. 10   H. 6
I. 7   J. 9   K. 6   L. 10
M. 10   N. 10   O. 8   P. 5
Q. 5   R. 8

Page 45

A. 4   B. 4   C. 2   D. 9   E. 4

Page 46

A. 3   B. 3   C. 2
D. 3   E. 2   F. 1
G. 3   H. 3   I. 3
Six stars should be colored.

Page 47

flower–orange   jacket–green
duck–yellow   boots–black
hat–red   puddle–blue

Page 48

Each fact family should be completed.

Page 49

A. 5   B. 9   C. 9   D. 6
E. 7   F. 10   G. 6   H. 9
I. 6   J. 10   K. 6   L. 10

Page 50

A1. Frances   A2. Jane   A3. 15
B1. 3   B2. 9   B3. 18   B4. 27

Page 51

A. 40   B. 94   C. 100   D. 59
E. 93   F. 99   G. 78   H. 67
I. 96   J. 66   K. 27   L. 48
D

Page 52

A. 60   B. 51   C. 0   D. 19
E. 10   F. 50   G. 16   H. 12
I. 53   J. 47   K. 13   L. 10

Page 53

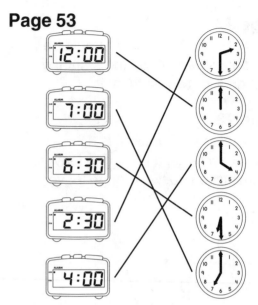

Page 54

A. 3:00   B. 1:30   C. 10:00
D. 6:00   E. 9:30   F. 8:00

Page 55

1. Wednesday   2. 5   3. Tuesday

Page 56

1. 4   2. 2   3. 5   4. 12

Page 57

The graph should be completed.

Page 58

1. Jan.: 7, Feb.: 6, Nov.: 1   2. 22 days

Page 59

The circle, square, and diamond should be circled.

Page 60

Shapes should be colored per directions.

Follow the directions in each box.

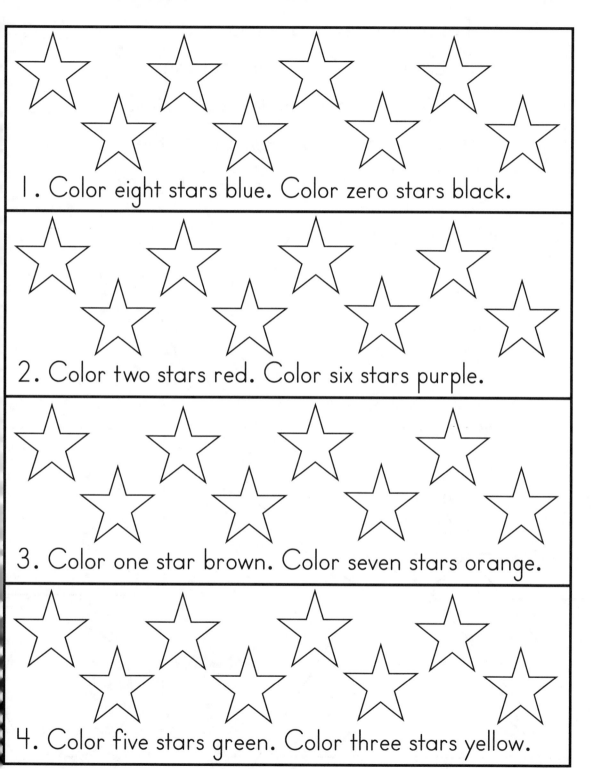

1. Color eight stars blue. Color zero stars black.

2. Color two stars red. Color six stars purple.

3. Color one star brown. Color seven stars orange.

4. Color five stars green. Color three stars yellow.

Follow the directions.

1. Color one square red.
2. Draw an X on four rectangles.
3. Draw a face inside two circles.
4. Count the triangles. Write the total number inside each triangle.

Match each number word to the correct number.

zero	4
one	2
two	5
three	0
four	1
five	3

six	7
seven	10
eight	9
nine	6
ten	8

Connect the dots from O to 50. Start at the ★. Color the picture.

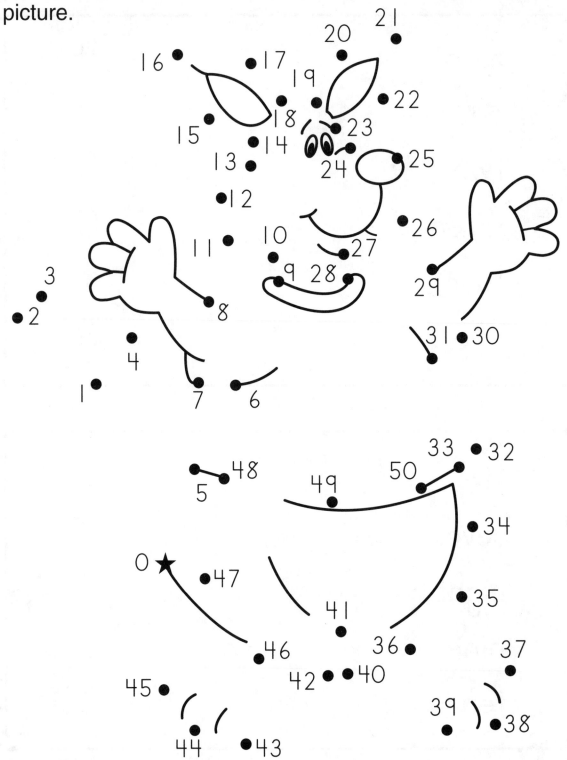

Write the missing numbers.

1	2	3				7			10
11				15		17			
			24				28	29	
	32	33			36				
					46	47	48		
51			54						60
		63		65				69	70
71	72				76	77			
	82		84	85					
		93				97	98		

Write the missing numbers.

A. _____, 7, _____

B. _____, 21, _____

C. _____, 34, _____

D. _____, 59, _____

E. _____, 63, _____

F. _____, 72, _____

G. _____, 47, 48

H. _____, 61, 62

I. _____, 13, 14

J. _____, 88, 89

K. _____, 94, 95

L. _____, 36, 37

M. 6, _____, 8

N. 81, _____, 83

O. 44, _____, 46

P. 79, _____, 81

Q. 25, _____, 27

R. 98, _____, 100

Write the missing numbers. Look for the pattern in each row.

A. 3, 4, _____, _____, 7, _____, _____

B. 5, 10, 15, _____, _____, 30, _____, 40

C. 4, 6, 8, _____, _____, 14, _____, 18

D. 46, 47, _____, 49, _____, _____, 52

E. 1, 3, 5, _____, _____, 11, 13, _____

F. 10, 20, _____, 40, _____, _____, 70

G. 3, 6, 9, _____, _____, 18, 21, _____

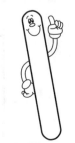

Fill in the circle next to the picture that comes next in each pattern.

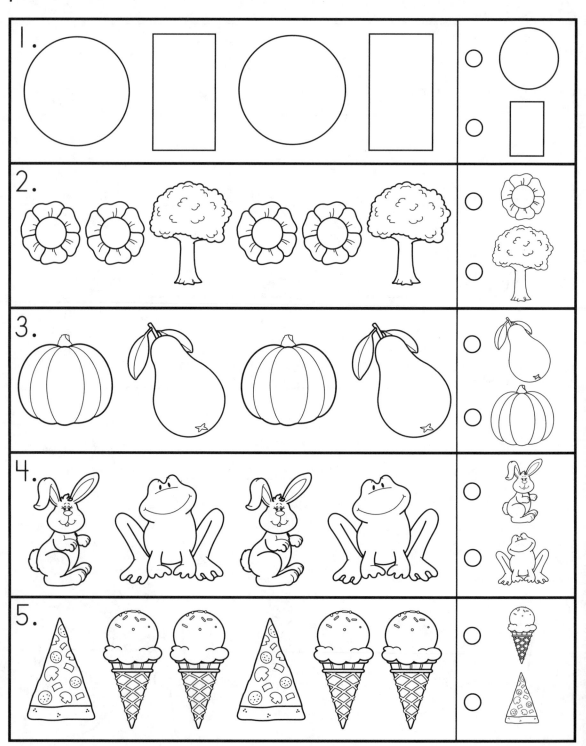

Draw a line from each fish to the word that shows its place in line.

fourth   fifth   first   second   third

Color the fish using the directions below.

1. Color the third fish red.
2. Color the first fish orange.
3. Color the second fish purple.
4. Color the fifth fish green.
5. Color the fourth fish yellow.

On the line below each box, write the number the box shows.

tens	ones
3	4

tens	ones
5	1

A. _____

B. _____

tens	ones
7	7

tens	ones
1	3

C. _____

D. _____

tens	ones
6	8

tens	ones
8	0

E. _____

F. _____

Write greater than (>) or less than (<) on each line.

A. 10 ___ 11   B. 44 ___ 43

C. 34 ___ 51   D. 59 ___ 61

E. 63 ___ 41   F. 72 ___ 70

G. 19 ___ 21   H. 86 ___ 76

I. 27 ___ 25   J. 91 ___ 78

K. 49 ___ 52   L. 33 ___ 28

M. 17 ___ 11   N. 89 ___ 98

O. 72 ___ 80   P. 46 ___ 38

Solve the problems. Use the pictures to help you.

A.
$$3$$
$$+ 3$$
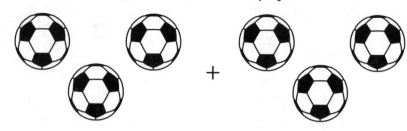

B.
$$7$$
$$+ 2$$

C.
$$5$$
$$+ 5$$
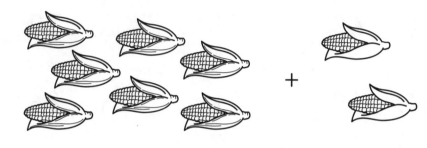

D.
$$1$$
$$+ 6$$

E.
$$8$$
$$+ 2$$

Solve the problems. Color all of the suns that have a sum of 9. How many did you color? _____

A.

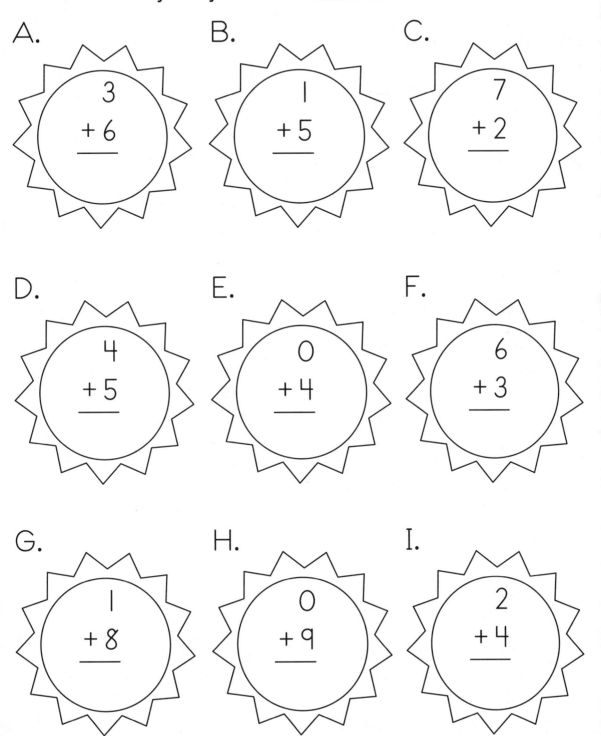

$$\begin{array}{r} 3 \\ +\ 6 \\ \hline \end{array}$$

B.

$$\begin{array}{r} 1 \\ +\ 5 \\ \hline \end{array}$$

C.

$$\begin{array}{r} 7 \\ +\ 2 \\ \hline \end{array}$$

D.

$$\begin{array}{r} 4 \\ +\ 5 \\ \hline \end{array}$$

E.

$$\begin{array}{r} 0 \\ +\ 4 \\ \hline \end{array}$$

F.

$$\begin{array}{r} 6 \\ +\ 3 \\ \hline \end{array}$$

G.

$$\begin{array}{r} 1 \\ +\ 8 \\ \hline \end{array}$$

H.

$$\begin{array}{r} 0 \\ +\ 9 \\ \hline \end{array}$$

I.

$$\begin{array}{r} 2 \\ +\ 4 \\ \hline \end{array}$$

How many addition problems can you solve correctly in two minutes?

A. 3
    +4
    ___

B. 7
    +1
    ___

C. 2
    +2
    ___

D. 3
    +3
    ___

E. 7
    +2
    ___

F. 4
    +2
    ___

G. 4
    +6
    ___

H. 6
    +0
    ___

I. 6
    +1
    ___

J. 3
    +6
    ___

K. 1
    +5
    ___

L. 5
    +5
    ___

M. 9
    +1
    ___

N. 10
    + 0
    ___

O. 6
    +2
    ___

P. 2
    +3
    ___

Q. 3
    +2
    ___

R. 3
    +5
    ___

Solve the problems. Use the pictures to help you.

A. $\begin{array}{r} 8 \\ -4 \\ \hline \end{array}$

B. $\begin{array}{r} 6 \\ -2 \\ \hline \end{array}$

C. $\begin{array}{r} 3 \\ -1 \\ \hline \end{array}$

D. $\begin{array}{r} 9 \\ -0 \\ \hline \end{array}$

E. $\begin{array}{r} 7 \\ -3 \\ \hline \end{array}$

Solve the problems. Color all of the stars that have a difference of 3. How many did you color? _____

A.

8
- 5
___

B.

6
- 3
___

C.

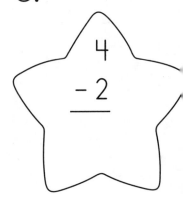

4
- 2
___

D.

3
- 0
___

E.

7
- 5
___

F.

2
- 1
___

G.

9
- 6
___

H.

5
- 2
___

I.

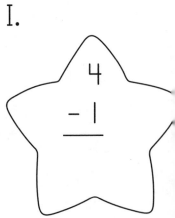

4
- 1
___

Solve the problems and color the picture using the key.

Key

2 = red   5 = green   4 = blue

8 = yellow   3 = orange   6 = black

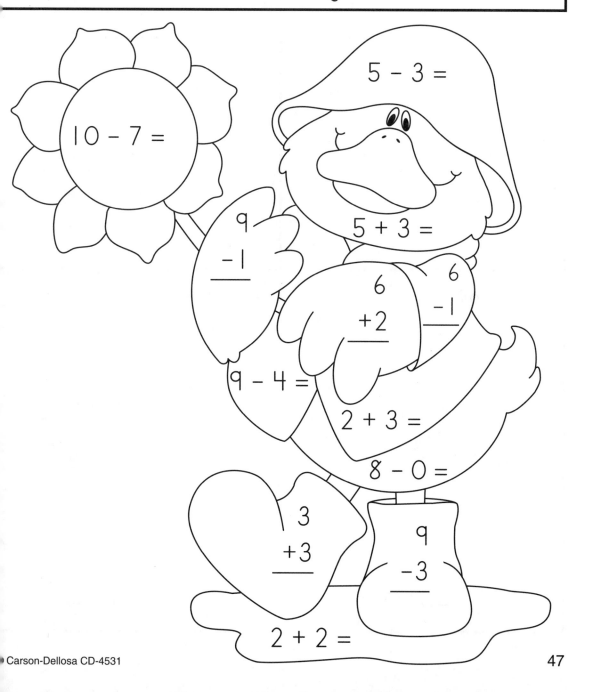

10 – 7 =

5 – 3 =

$\begin{array}{r} 9 \\ -1 \\ \hline \end{array}$

5 + 3 =

$\begin{array}{r} 6 \\ +2 \\ \hline \end{array}$

$\begin{array}{r} 6 \\ -1 \\ \hline \end{array}$

9 – 4 =

2 + 3 =

8 – 0 =

$\begin{array}{r} 3 \\ +3 \\ \hline \end{array}$

$\begin{array}{r} 9 \\ -3 \\ \hline \end{array}$

2 + 2 =

Write the missing numbers in each fact family.

A. family: 5, 3, 2

$2 + 3 =$ _____

$3 +$ _____ $= 5$

$5 -$ _____ $= 2$

$5 - 2 =$ _____

B. family: 10, 6, 4

$6 +$ _____ $= 10$

$4 +$ _____ $= 10$

$10 - 6 =$ _____

_____ $- 4 = 6$

C. family: 7, 4, 3

_____ $+ 3 = 7$

$3 + 4 =$ _____

$7 -$ _____ $= 4$

$7 -$ _____ $= 3$

D. family: 3, 2, 1

$2 + 1 =$ _____

_____ $+ 2 = 3$

_____ $- 1 = 2$

$3 - 2 =$ _____

Solve the problems.

A.
$$\begin{array}{r} 2 \\ 3 \\ +\,0 \\ \hline \end{array}$$

B.
$$\begin{array}{r} 5 \\ 1 \\ +\,3 \\ \hline \end{array}$$

C.
$$\begin{array}{r} 6 \\ 2 \\ +\,1 \\ \hline \end{array}$$

D.
$$\begin{array}{r} 4 \\ 0 \\ +\,2 \\ \hline \end{array}$$

E.
$$\begin{array}{r} 0 \\ 6 \\ +\,1 \\ \hline \end{array}$$

F.
$$\begin{array}{r} 4 \\ 3 \\ +\,3 \\ \hline \end{array}$$

G.
$$\begin{array}{r} 3 \\ 1 \\ +\,2 \\ \hline \end{array}$$

H.
$$\begin{array}{r} 3 \\ 3 \\ +\,3 \\ \hline \end{array}$$

I.
$$\begin{array}{r} 2 \\ 2 \\ +\,2 \\ \hline \end{array}$$

J.
$$\begin{array}{r} 8 \\ 1 \\ +\,1 \\ \hline \end{array}$$

K.
$$\begin{array}{r} 1 \\ 5 \\ +\,0 \\ \hline \end{array}$$

L.
$$\begin{array}{r} 0 \\ 4 \\ +\,6 \\ \hline \end{array}$$

Read the story problems and answer the questions.

A. Frances had 8 cookies. Jane had 3 cookies. Carla had 4 cookies.

1. Who had the most cookies? _____

2. Who had the fewest cookies? _____

3. How many cookies did they have in all?

_____

B. I cleaned my room. I found 3 sweaters and 6 shirts. There were 10 socks. I also found 8 shoes.

1. How many sweaters did I find? _____

2. How many sweaters and shirts were there in all? _____

3. How many shoes and socks were there in all?

_____

4. How many things did I find in all? _____

Solve the problems.

A.
$$
\begin{array}{r}
30 \\
+\ 10 \\
\hline
\end{array}
$$

B.
$$
\begin{array}{r}
90 \\
+\ \ 4 \\
\hline
\end{array}
$$

C.
$$
\begin{array}{r}
50 \\
+\ 50 \\
\hline
\end{array}
$$

D.
$$
\begin{array}{r}
34 \\
+\ 25 \\
\hline
\end{array}
$$

E.
$$
\begin{array}{r}
51 \\
+\ 42 \\
\hline
\end{array}
$$

F.
$$
\begin{array}{r}
77 \\
+\ 22 \\
\hline
\end{array}
$$

G.
$$
\begin{array}{r}
62 \\
+\ 16 \\
\hline
\end{array}
$$

H.
$$
\begin{array}{r}
46 \\
+\ 21 \\
\hline
\end{array}
$$

I.
$$
\begin{array}{r}
85 \\
+\ 11 \\
\hline
\end{array}
$$

J.
$$
\begin{array}{r}
33 \\
+\ 33 \\
\hline
\end{array}
$$

K.
$$
\begin{array}{r}
14 \\
+\ 13 \\
\hline
\end{array}
$$

L.
$$
\begin{array}{r}
28 \\
+\ 20 \\
\hline
\end{array}
$$

Solve the problems.

A.
$$\begin{array}{r} 90 \\ -\ 30 \\ \hline \end{array}$$

B.
$$\begin{array}{r} 76 \\ -\ 25 \\ \hline \end{array}$$

C.
$$\begin{array}{r} 83 \\ -\ 83 \\ \hline \end{array}$$

D.
$$\begin{array}{r} 59 \\ -\ 40 \\ \hline \end{array}$$

E.
$$\begin{array}{r} 29 \\ -\ 19 \\ \hline \end{array}$$

F.
$$\begin{array}{r} 60 \\ -\ 10 \\ \hline \end{array}$$

G.
$$\begin{array}{r} 47 \\ -\ 31 \\ \hline \end{array}$$

H.
$$\begin{array}{r} 15 \\ -\ 3 \\ \hline \end{array}$$

I.
$$\begin{array}{r} 75 \\ -\ 22 \\ \hline \end{array}$$

J.
$$\begin{array}{r} 98 \\ -\ 51 \\ \hline \end{array}$$

K.
$$\begin{array}{r} 36 \\ -\ 23 \\ \hline \end{array}$$

L.
$$\begin{array}{r} 54 \\ -\ 44 \\ \hline \end{array}$$

Draw a line from each clock to a clock with the same time.

Write the time you see on each clock. Trace the first one that has been done for you.

A.

3:00
_____

B.

_____

C.

_____

D.

_____

E.

_____

F.

_____

Write the dates on the calendar and answer the questions.

			October			
Sun.	Mon.	Tues.	Wed.	Thurs.	Fri.	Sat.
	1					
						13
			31			

1. On what day of the week does October end?

   _____

   _____

2. How many Mondays are in October?

   _____

   _____

3. What day of the week is October 23?

   _____

   _____

Read the graph and answer the questions.

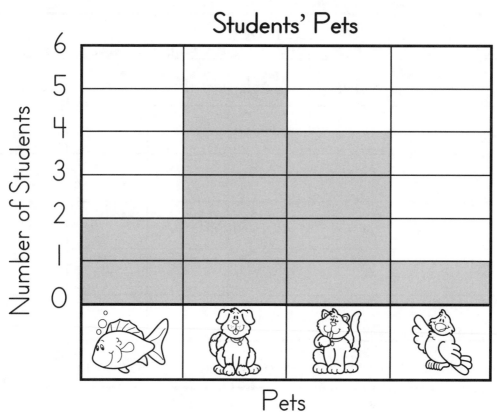

Students' Pets

1. How many students have a cat? _____

2. How many students have a fish? _____

3. How many students have a dog? _____

4. How many students in all have pets? _____

56

Use the chart below to fill in the bar graph.

pizza	卌
hot dogs	lll
chicken	ll
spaghetti	卌 l

Favorite Foods

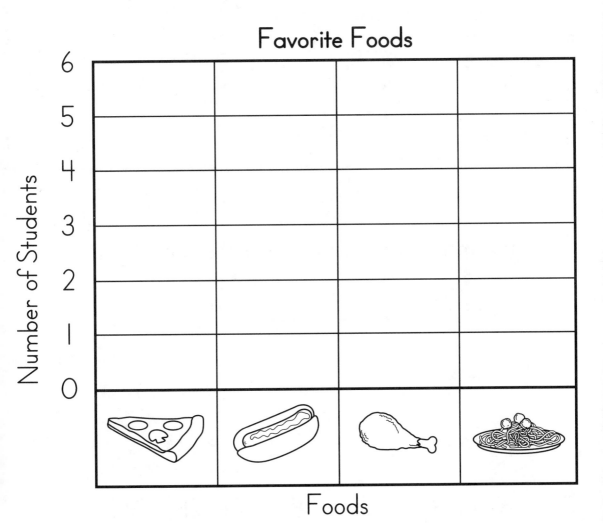

Number of Students

6
5
4
3
2
1
0

Foods

Read the graph and answer the questions.

Snowy Days in Winter

Months	Number of Snowy Days
November	❄
December	❄ ❄ ❄ ❄ ❄ ❄
January	❄ ❄ ❄ ❄ ❄ ❄ ❄
February	❄ ❄ ❄ ❄ ❄ ❄
March	❄ ❄

❄ = 1 snowy day

1. How many snowy days were there in:

   January? _____

   February? _____

   November? _____

2. How many days in all did it snow in winter? _____

58

Circle all of the shapes that are divided in half.

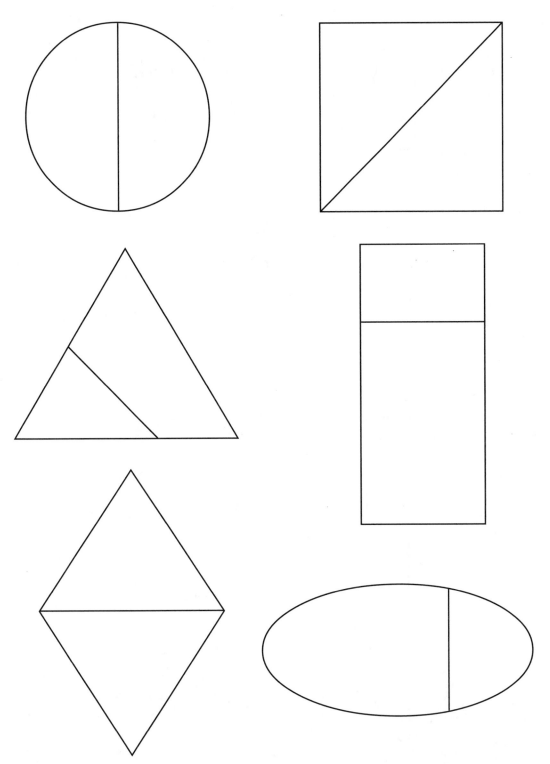

Follow the directions next to each shape.

A.
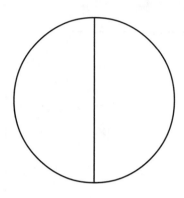
Color $\frac{1}{2}$ red.

Color $\frac{1}{2}$ blue.

B.
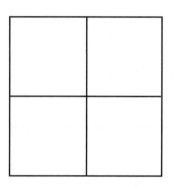
Color $\frac{1}{4}$ green.

Color $\frac{1}{4}$ yellow.

Color $\frac{1}{4}$ orange.

Color $\frac{1}{4}$ purple.

C.
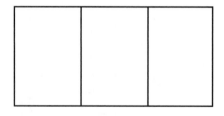
Color $\frac{1}{3}$ blue.

Color $\frac{1}{3}$ yellow.

Color $\frac{1}{3}$ green.

D.
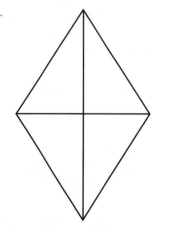
Color $\frac{1}{4}$ orange.

Color $\frac{1}{4}$ red.

Color $\frac{1}{2}$ purple.